HAPPY BIRTHDAY
Bagpuss

With easy projects to make

COLLINS & BROWN

Based on the Bagpuss films made by Oliver Postgate and Peter Firmin, as Smallfilms, for the BBC.

Story by Kate Haxell using illustrations, projects and written material from the Bagpuss albums. Additional new illustrations by Peter Firmin.

Contents

This book belongs to

In 1973, Bagpuss was an idea for a 'marmalade' cat who entertained children by showing them pictures in a 'thinks bubble'. Oliver Postgate had memories of sleeping cats in old-fashioned shops, so, as the BBC had asked Smallfilms for a new series, we decided to give Bagpuss his own shop.

Who could run it? My daughter Emily was the right age. She agreed and Joan, my wife, made her a dress. What would they sell? Oliver said they don't sell anything... they mend toys!

Emily and Bagpuss needed help so more characters were added. Oliver suggested a 'Mouse Organ' to play the music. Joan had made Madeleine the rag-doll as a nighty case. Gabriel the banjo-playing toad would play folk songs.

We needed a wise character who would know everything! The BBC did not care for my first suggestion, Professor Bogwood, so a wooden woodpecker called Professor Yaffle took his place. We finally had our cast and now I had to make them.

The special striped cloth I ordered for Emily's marmalade cat turned out to be pink by some fortunate accident, and so Bagpuss became the pink and cream cat that we all know: the most important, the most beautiful, the most magical, saggy old cloth cat in the whole wide world.

With John Faulkner and Sandra Kerr to sing and Oliver narrating and speaking for Bagpuss and Professor Yaffle, we made thirteen films which were first shown in 1974.

So it is now Bagpuss's 40th birthday and we wanted to make him some presents. In this book you will find instructions to make them yourself.

We hope you will have as much fun making them as we did making the films 40 years ago.

Peter Firmin

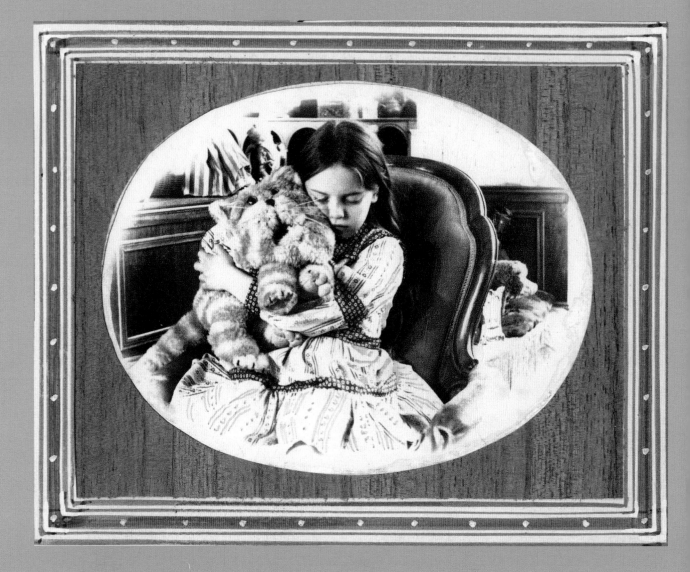

Here is a picture of Emily and Bagpuss.
Emily thinks Bagpuss is the most beautiful,
most important and most magical cat in the
whole wide world, but you may think he
looks like a saggy old cloth cat.

Here is Emily's shop, where Bagpuss and his friends live. Most of the time Bagpuss sleeps in the shop window, but when Emily brings him something to look at, she only has to say a few magic words...

Bagpuss dear Catpuss

These are the magic words that Emily says to wake Bagpuss up...

'Bagpuss, dear Bagpuss, old furry catpuss,
Wake up and look at this thing that I bring.

Wake up, be bright! Be golden and light!
Bagpuss, oh hear what I sing.'

To cross-stitch a catpuss message for Bagpuss you will need...

Fabric such as even-weave linen (used here) or Aida. The chart is 116 stitches across and 72 stitches high, so the fabric needs to be large enough to fit that in, plus some extra for framing the embroidery (see page 10).

Stranded embroidery thread in two shades of pink

Chart on page 11

Embroidery needle

Embroidery hoop

Ribbon for hanging (optional)

Embroidery

Fit the fabric into the hoop. Make each cross stitch over either two threads of linen, or one thread of Aida. Make the stitches the same, so that the top stitch of each cross slopes in the same direction. You can make diagonal stitches in one direction right across a row, then work back making the second stitch to complete the cross.

Framing

You can frame the cross stitch in the hoop you used to embroider it. Leave the embroidery in the hoop and tighten the hoop screw as much as possible. Trim the excess fabric into a circle at least 5cm larger all around than the hoop. Sew gathering stitches around the edge of the circle.

Finishing

Pull the stitches up tight at the back and fasten off the thread. You can sew on a circle of felt to cover the hole in the back if you want to. Tie a piece of ribbon around the screw to hang the framed embroidery from.

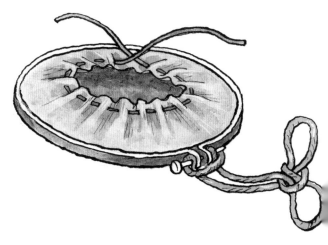

A Knitted Bagpuss

To knit a Bagpuss to blow out the birthday cake candles you will need...

YARN

2 x 25g balls of Rowan Angora Haze in each of Nest 523 (A) and Caress 525 (B), both used double throughout

Small amounts of black and white DK yarns

NEEDLES

Pair of 3.5mm knitting needles

OTHER MATERIALS

Tapestry needle

Toy stuffing

TENSION

An exact tension is not necessary for this project

SIZE

37cm long (including tail) by 27cm wide (including legs)

Abbreviations

alt = alternate

beg = begin(ning)

cont = continue

dec = decrease

foll(s) = follow(ing)(s)

inc = increase

k = knit

k2tog = knit two stitches together

m1 = make one (pick up bar between stitches and work through back loop)

p = purl

p2tog = purl two stitches together

p2togtbl = purl two stitches together through back loop

pm = place marker

rem = remain(ing)

rep = repeat

RH = right hand

RS = right side

skpo = slip1, knit 1, pass the slipped stitch over

sk2po = slip1, knit 2 together, pass the slipped stitch over

sm = slip marker

st(s) = stitch(es)

st st = stocking stitch

WS = wrong side

Pattern

Tummy

Using A, cast on 43 sts.

Row 1 (RS): K20, m1, k3, m1, k20. (45 sts)

Row 2 and every foll alt row: Purl.

Row 3: K20, m1, k5, m1, k20. (47 sts)

Row 5: K20, m1, k7, m1, k20. (49 sts)

Row 7: K20, m1, k9, m1, k20. (51 sts)

Row 9: K20, m1, k11, m1, k20. (53 sts)

Row 11: K20, m1, k13, m1, k20. (55 sts)

Row 13: K20, m1, k15, m1, k20. (57 sts)

Row 15: K20, m1, k17, m1, k20. (59 sts)

Row 16: Purl.

Shape back legs

Cast off 3 sts at beg of next 6 rows. (41 sts)

Shape tummy

Work 4 rows straight.

Dec 1 st at each end of next and foll 4th row. (37 sts)

Work 3 rows straight.

Cast off 2 sts at beg of next 2 rows. (33 sts)

Dec 1 st at each end of next and foll 6 alt rows. (19 sts)

Purl 1 row.

Neck and shoulders

Next row: K4, turn.

Next row: P4.

Next row: K2, k2tog, turn.

Next row: P3.

Cast off.

Rejoin yarn to rem sts.

Cast off next 11 sts, k to end.

Complete to match first side, reversing shapings.

Back

*Using B, cast on 24 sts.

Inc 1 st at each end of next and foll alt row. (28 sts)

Purl 1 row.*

Break yarn and push sts to end of needle.

Rep from * to * once more.

Next row: Inc in first st, knit to last st of this section, knit this st tog with first st of first section, knit to last st of this section, inc in last st. (57 sts)

Next row: Purl.

Join in A, do not break B.

Work 6 rows st st in A.

Work 6 rows st st in B.

Keeping stripe sequence as set, cont as folls:

Shape back legs

Cast off 3 sts at beg of next 6 rows. (39 sts)

Shape back

Row 1 (RS): K19, m1, k1, m1, k19. (41 sts)

Row 2 and every foll alt row: Purl.

Row 3: K19, m1, k3, m1, k19. (43 sts)

Row 5: K19, m1, k5, m1, k19. (45 sts)

Row 7: K19, m1, k7, m1, k19. (47 sts)

Row 9: K19, m1, k9, m1, k19. (49 sts)

Row 11: K19, m1, k11, m1, k19. (51 sts)

Row 13: K19, m1, k13, m1, k19. (53 sts)

Row 14: Purl.

Shape armhole

Next row: Cast off 4 sts, k until there are 15 sts on RH needle, m1, k15, m1, k to end. (51 sts)

Next row: Cast off 4 sts, purl to end. (47 sts)

Next row: Skpo, k until there are 14 sts on RH needle, skpo, k13, k2tog, k to last 2 sts, k2tog. (43 sts)

Next row and every foll alt row: Purl.

Next row: Skpo, k until there are 13 sts on RH needle, skpo, k11, k2tog, k to last 2 sts, k2tog. (39 sts)

Next row: Skpo, k until there are 12 sts on RH needle, skpo, k9, k2tog, k to last 2 sts, k2tog. (35 sts)

Next row: Skpo, k until there are 11 sts on RH needle, skpo, k7, k2tog, k to last 2 sts, k2tog. (31 sts)

Next row: Skpo, k until there are 10 sts on RH needle, skpo, k5, k2tog, k to last 2 sts, k2tog. (27 sts)

Next row: Skpo, k until there are 9 sts on RH needle, skpo, k3, k2tog, k to last 2 sts, k2tog. (23 sts)

Next row: Skpo, k until there are 8 sts on RH needle, skpo, k1, k2tog, k to last 2 sts, k2tog. (19 sts)

Next row: Purl.

Neck and shoulders

Next row: K4, turn.

Next row: P4.

Next row: K2, k2tog, turn.

Next row: P3.

Cast off.

Rejoin yarn to rem sts.

Cast off next 11 sts, k to end.

Complete to match first side, reversing shapings.

Chin and Face

Pick up and knit 11 sts from cast-off edge at top of Tummy in B.

Next row (WS): Inc in every st across the row. (22 sts)

Next row: [Inc in next st, k1] to end. (33 sts)

Next row: Purl.

Join in A and cont in stripe sequence as previously set.

Cast on 2 sts at beg of next 4 rows. (41 sts)

Work 8 rows straight.

Next row: K11, pm, k to last 11 sts, pm, k11.

Next row: P11, sm, p to last 11 sts, sm, p11.

Next row: K to marker, sm, m1, k to next marker, m1, sm, k to end. (43 sts)

Next row: P11, sm, p to last 11 sts, sm, p11.

Rep last 2 rows, 4 more times. (51 sts)

Work 18 rows straight.

Next row: K to marker, sm, skpo, k to 2 sts before next marker, k2tog, sm, k to end. (49 sts)

Next row: P11, sm, p to last 11 sts, sm, p11.

Rep last 2 rows, 3 more times. (43 sts)

Next row: K11, sm, skpo, k to 2 sts before next marker, k2tog, sm, k11. (41 sts)

Next row: P11, sm, p2tog, p to 2 sts before next marker, p2togtbl, sm, p11. (39 sts)

Cont to dec as set on the next 6 rows. (27 sts)

Next row: K to 2 sts before marker, skpo, sm, skpo, k1, k2tog, sm, k2tog, k to end. (23 sts)

Next row: P to 2 sts before marker, p2tog, sm, p3, sm, p2togtbl, p to end. (21 sts)

Next row: K to 2 sts before marker, skpo, sm, k3, sm, k2tog, k to end. (19 sts)

Next row: P to 2 sts before marker, p2tog, sm, p3, sm, p2togtbl, p to end. (17 sts)

Rep last 2 rows twice more. (9 sts)

Next row: Purl.

Next row: Skpo, k5, k2tog. (7 sts)

Cast off.

Back of head

Pick up and knit 12 sts along cast-off edge at top of Back in B.

Work in stripe sequence as previously set for 8 rows.

Inc 1 st at each end of next and every foll alt row to 24 sts.

Next row: Purl.

Cast off.

Front legs

Using B, cast on 30 sts.

Work 6 rows st st in B.

Join in A, do not break B.

Work 6 rows st st in A.

Rep last 12 rows once more.

Break A.

Next row: K11, [m1, k1] 4 times, [k1, m1] 4 times, k11. (38 sts)

Next row: P15, [inc in next st] 8 times, p15. (46 sts)

Work 3 rows straight.

Cast off.

Tail

Using B, cast on 17 sts.

Work 6 rows st st in B.

Join in A, do not break B.

Work 6 rows st st in A.

Rep last 12 rows twice more and then first 6 rows once more.

Break B.

Dec 1 st at each end of next 6 rows. (5 sts)

Cast off.

Front paw pads (make 2)

Using A, cast on 11 sts.

Work in garter st throughout.

Knit 2 rows.

Inc 1 st at each end of next and foll alt row. (15 sts)

Work 13 rows straight, ending with RS facing for next row.

Dec 1 st at each end of next and foll 3 alt rows. (7 sts)

Knit 1 row.

Cast off.

Back paw pads (make 2)

Using A, cast on 5 sts.

Work in garter st throughout.

Knit 2 rows.

Inc 1 st at each end of next and foll alt row. (9 sts)

Work 9 rows straight, ending with RS facing for next row.

Dec 1 st at each end of next and foll alt row. (5 sts)

Knit 1 row.

Cast off.

Ears

Using A, cast on 11 sts.

Knit 3 rows.

Next row (RS): Dec 1 st at each end of row.

Rep last row until 3 sts rem.

Next row: Sk2po, fasten off.

Muzzle

Using A, cast on 4 sts.

Work in garter st throughout.

Knit 14 rows.

Next row (RS): K1, m1, k to last st, m1, k1. (6 sts)

Knit 5 rows.

Next row: K1, m1, k to last st, m1, k1. (8 sts)

Knit 3 rows.

Rep last 4 rows, 4 times more. (16 sts)

Next row: K1, m1, k to last st, m1, k1. (18 sts)

Knit 1 row.

Rep last 2 rows once more. (20 sts)

Knit 2 rows.

Next row: K1, skpo, k to last 3 sts, k2tog, k1. (18 sts)

Knit 1 row.

Rep last 2 rows, 3 times more. (12 sts)

Next row: Cast off, working k1, skpo, k to last 3 sts, k2tog, k1.

Finishing

Weave in any loose ends.

Press according to ball band instructions if necessary.

With right sides facing, join cast-on edges of Back and Tummy with backstitch.

Back legs

Pick up and knit 22 sts in B from edge of leg.

Next row: Purl, inc 8 sts evenly across the row. (30 sts)

Work 3 rows straight.

Cast off.

Starting at cast-off edge for Back Legs, join side seams to base of armhole with backstitch. Sew in back paw pads.

Join shoulder seams.

Join back seam of Front Legs with backstitch and while work is still inside out, stitch paw pads into place. Turn RS out.

Sew front legs into armholes.

Stuff body.

Stitch sides of head so that they meet the sts cast off at the top of the Back.

Stuff head and then join sides of back of head to sides of face with mattress st and sew cast-off edge to meet cast-off edge at top of head, pulling excess fabric to a peak which forms the inner ear.

Stitch ears into place behind these peaks.

Sew muzzle to face using blanket stitch, matching cast-on edge to top of tummy. Using black yarn and chain stitch, embroider eyes and nose, and use backstitch for mouth. Use black yarn and French knots for whisker marks, and white yarn for eye highlights.

Join seam on tail. Stuff and sew in place.

The very first thing Bagpuss sees when he wakes up

is a wrapped gift Emily has brought him.

On the large tag tied to the ribbon she had written...

Happy Birthday
Bagpuss
Old Furry Catpuss

When Bagpuss wakes up, all his friends wake up, too. They all gathered around to look at the beautifully wrapped parcel.

'Oh my,' said Eddiemouse.

'It's Bagpuss's birthday and Emily has brought him a gift.'

'But we don't have a gift to give,' cried Janiemouse.

'We must get a gift for Bagpuss.'

'Yes,' said Madeleine.

'We must all give Bagpuss something lovely for his special birthday.'

'We have lots of money,' said Yaffle.

'We can buy Bagpuss a gift. Look, these coins are from Ancient Greece, we can buy something very magnificent with these.'

'Those coins are no good today,' cried Charliemouse.

'We can't spend those in a shop.'

'Wait a minute,' said Eddiemouse.

'We are IN a shop. Let's hunt in here for a gift to give.

Look everywhere!

Is there a gift on the next page?'

'We could give Bagpuss this embroidered cloth,' said Madeleine.

'It is very beautiful, and very old.

Do you think that it is beautiful enough for a birthday gift?'

'That,' said Professor Yaffle, 'Is a genuine antique, and...

But then Jenniemouse saw the embroidery and let out a shriek.

'It's an owl, an owl,' she cried.

'It will eat us all for its tea.'

And all the mice fled to hide behind the mouse organ.

'Well that's no good then,' said Madeleine. 'We can't give Bagpuss a gift that frightens all the mice so much.'

'How ridiculous,' muttered Yaffle. 'It's just an embroidery, just a picture...'

'Come out from there,'

said Madeleine to the mice.

'Don't be frightened. I have put the owl away. We will all MAKE gifts for Bagpuss; those will be the gifts he would like best of all.'

'What will we make?' cried the mice.

'Will you help us make a gift?'

'Yes,' said Madeleine. 'I will help everyone to make
a perfect birthday gift.' And she put on her apron.

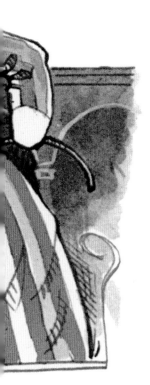

A Lavender Madeleine

'My birthday gift for Bagpuss will be a lavender me,' decided Madeleine.

'It will smell delicious, and be just as pretty as me.'

To make a sweet-smelling Madeleine you will need...

Pattern pieces on pages 26 and 27

Striped cotton fabric, 35 x 35cm (you can use different patterns or colours for the skirt and bodice if you want)

Cream cotton fabric, 20 x 10cm

Pencil

Fabric scissors

Scraps of white and blue felt

Ribbon, 16cm long

Chunky brown knitting yarn or rug wool

A little toy stuffing

Embroidery threads

Embroidery needle

Dried lavender

Sewing machine (though you can sew the seams by hand)

Sewing needle and thread

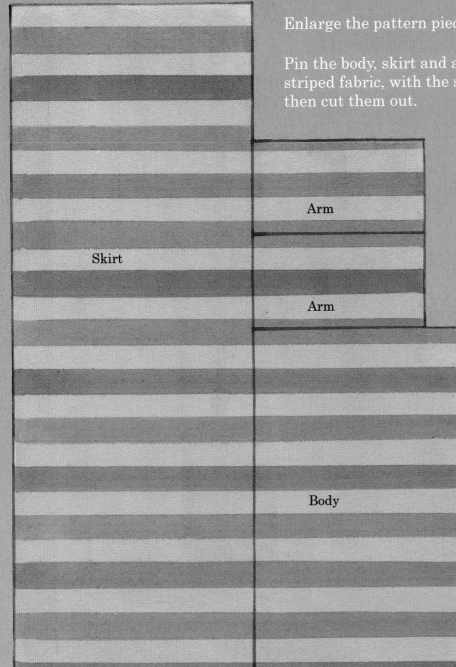

Enlarge the pattern pieces by 200%.

Pin the body, skirt and arm pattern pieces onto the striped fabric, with the stripes running as shown, then cut them out.

Arm

Arm

Skirt

Body

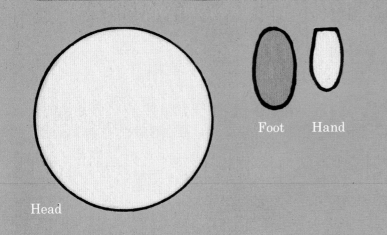

Head

Foot   Hand

Head

Cut out two heads from the cream cotton. On one circle, embroider the features: it's best to draw them on lightly with pencil or a fading fabric marker first, following the guide. Use backstitch or stem stitch to outline the eyes, and make the eyebrows and mouth. Make the irises from circles of chain stitch and the nose from French knots. Alternatively, draw the features on with coloured fibre-tipped pens.

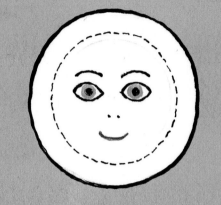

Put the two circles right sides together and sew around the edge, leaving a small gap at the top. Turn the head right side out and stuff, then sew up the gap.

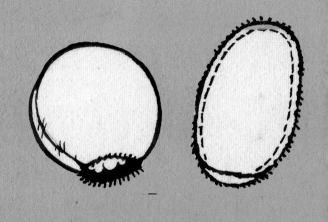

Hair

Cut pieces of yarn and twist them so that they form tight curls. Sew these onto the head, arranging them to make Madeleine's curly hair.

Madeleine stitched and stuffed and soon
her lavender self was done.

Body

Right sides together, fold the body piece in half to make a long tube with the stripes running round it. Sew up the long seam and one short seam. Turn the body right side out. Put the lavender into the bottom, and fill the body to the top with toy stuffing.

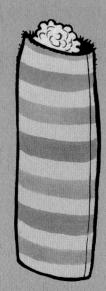

Arms

Fold each arm piece in half lengthways, right sides together, and sew up the long seam and one short seam. Turn the arms right side out and fill them with toy stuffing. Fold the open end diagonally, as shown, and sew up the opening.

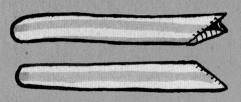

Skirt

Fold the skirt piece in half with right sides together and the stripes running up and down, and sew up the side seam. Turn under and sew a narrow hem around the bottom. Gather the top to fit around the middle of the body tube. Sew the ribbon on around the gathered top of the skirt, turning under the ends to neaten them.

Making up

Fold in the shoulders of the body
diagonally, as shown, and sew the arms
on. Sew the head to the top of the body.
Cut out four hand pieces and four foot
pieces from felt. Oversew them together
in pairs, stuffing them before you
complete the sewing. Sew the hands to
the ends of the arms and the feet to the
bottom of the body. Slide the skirt onto
the body to about two-thirds of the way
up, and sew it in place.

'Mice is nice!' shouted the mice.

'We want to make mice for Bagpuss!'

And they looked expectantly at Madeleine.

'All right mice,' said Madeleine.

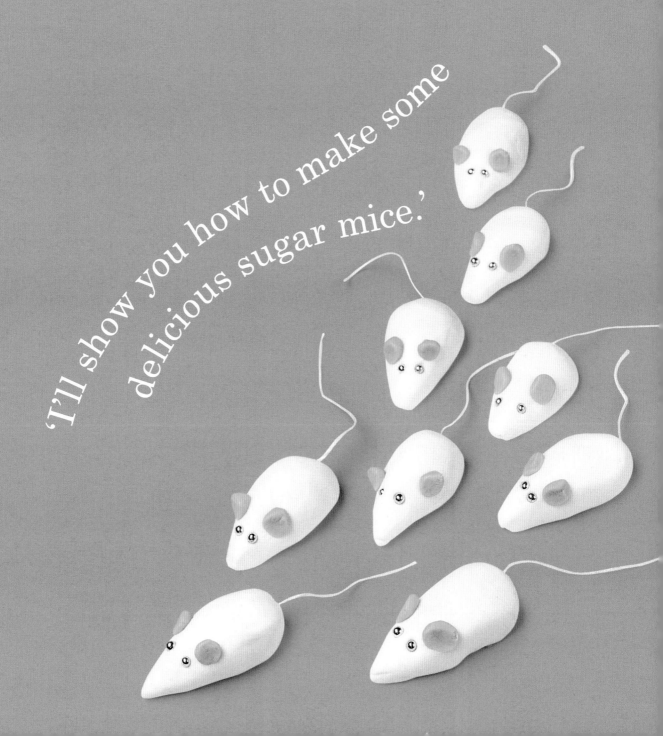

'I'll show you how to make some delicious sugar mice.'

Sugar Mice

Madeleine put on her apron while the mice brought...

225g of white icing sugar

One small egg (note that the mice contain raw egg white)

Half a lemon

A bottle of pink food colouring

Packet of edible silver ball cake decorations

White embroidery thread or string

Two bowls and a cup

A wooden spoon and a dessertspoon

A sieve and a lemon squeezer

First the mice sieved the icing sugar into a bowl.

Then Madeleine broke the egg and cleverly separated the white from the yolk by passing the yolk from one half of the eggshell to the other over a cup until only the yolk was left in the eggshell, and all the white had dropped into the cup.

Then the mice mixed the egg white and the icing sugar together with a wooden spoon and added lemon juice drop by drop until the mixture was soft and podgy, but not runny. (If your mixture is a bit runny, add some more icing sugar.)

They took one dessertspoonful of the mixture and put it into another bowl. Then they added pink colouring drop by drop until the mixture was pink all the way through.

The mice took lumps of the white mixture and rolled and pushed them into the shape of mice. They used tiny bits of the pink mixture for ears and silver balls for eyes.

For the tails they used pieces of embroidery thread stuck into the mixture.

When they were done they had a dozen white mice with pink ears lined up on a piece of greaseproof paper, and one small pink mouse with white ears because they had some pink mixture left over.

The real mice wanted to give the sugar mice to Bagpuss at once, but Madeleine said that they had to wait until the sugar mice were set, about three hours. Then they could give Bagpuss his birthday gift. In the meantime, she let them eat up the leftover silver balls.

How Many 'B's?

Can you find 40 things beginning with 'B' in this picture? The answers are on page 64.

Bagpuss and Friends

Here is a picture of Bagpuss and some of his friends for you to colour in.

A Beanbag Gabriel

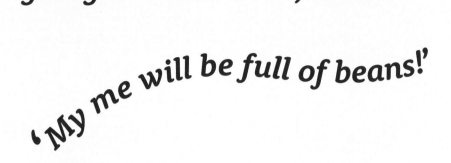

'For Bagpuss's birthday I'm going to make a me,' said Gabriel.

'My me will be full of beans!'

To make a banjo-playing beanbag Gabriel you will need...

Body pattern and banjo template on pages 40 and 41

Brushed cotton fabric, 36 x 29cm

Sewing machine (though you can sew the seams by hand)

Pins or sticky tape

Sewing needle and thread

Embroidery needle and black embroidery thread

A little toy stuffing or cotton wool

Dried lentils or rice

Buttons for eyes

Brown cardboard, 7 x 17cm

Tracing paper

Pencil

Sharp, small scissors

Black fibre-tipped pen

'What will the beans do?' cried the mice.
'What will they do?'

'They will let the beanbag me sit up and play the mini banjo I shall make!' said Gabriel happily.

Gabriel

Trace or photocopy the body patterns onto thin paper. There are two pieces: the longer one (to A) is the top and the shorter one (to B) is the bottom. Cut the patterns out.

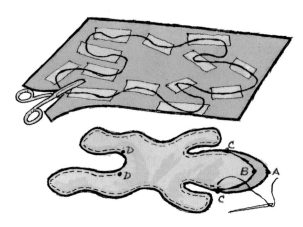

Pin or tape the body patterns to the fabric and cut them out. Pin the fabric pieces right sides together and sew around each edge from C to D, taking out the pins as you go.

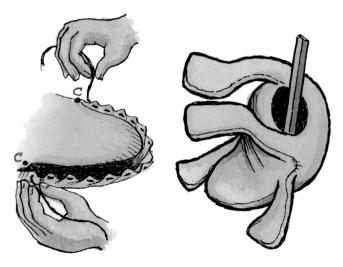

Run a line of gathering stitches around the longer nose on the top body piece, from C to A to C, and pull the stitches up until the nose matches the shorter one. Sew the noses together around the edges.

Turn the body right side out through the gap from D to D. Use a chopstick or knitting needle to push out the hands and feet. Stuff the arms and head with toy stuffing or cotton wool. Holding Gabriel upside down, fill him tightly with lentils or rice, then sew up the gap. Push some of the filling down into his legs.

Pinch a ridge across the top of his head and sew it in two places, where the eyes will be. Using black thread, sew on two four-hole white buttons to make his eyes.

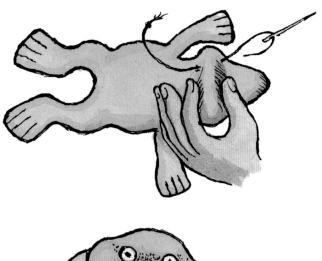

Thread the embroidery needle with black embroidery thread, and sew three lines on each hand to make fingers, so Gabriel can play his banjo. Sew lines on his feet, too. Now Gabriel needs his banjo!

Banjo

Using the pencil, trace the banjo template. Put the tracing pencil-side down on the cardboard and scribble over the back of it to transfer the lines onto the cardboard. Draw over the lines with the fibre-tipped pen, then cut out the banjo.

Sit Gabriel up with his banjo. Now he is happy!

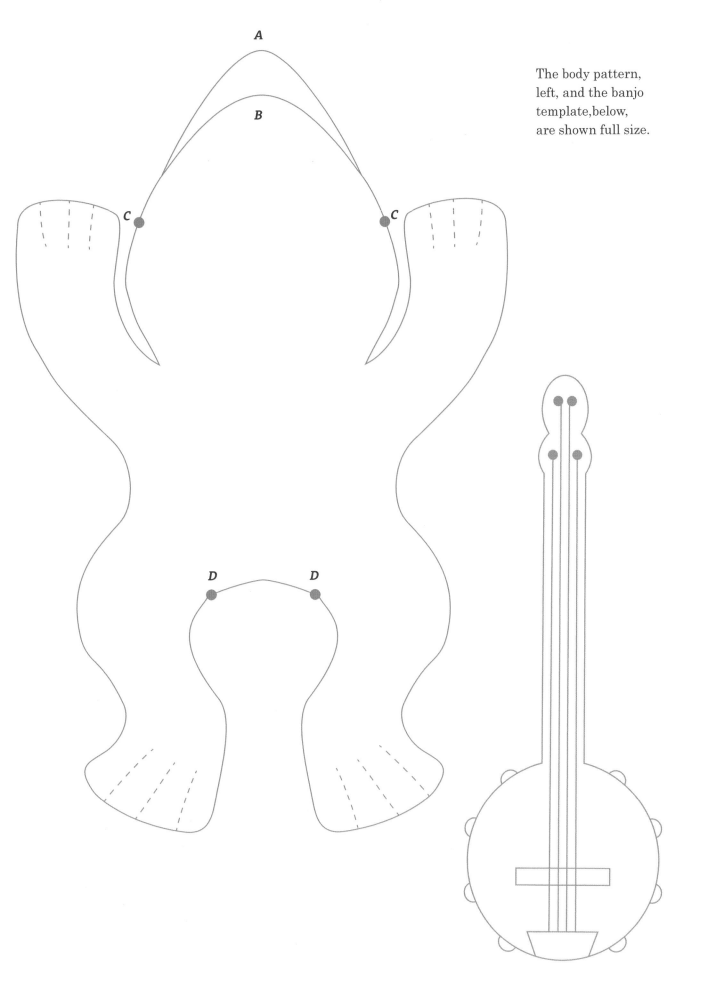

A

B

C *C*

D *D*

The body pattern, left, and the banjo template, below, are shown full size.

41

'We should give the shop a spring clean for Bagpuss's birthday,' said Madeleine.

'We should dust and polish everything, even the highest, darkest corners.'

'We can do that,' shouted the mice, as they ran to fetch mops and buckets. 'We can clean everything,' they shouted, as they ran in with scrubbing brushes and soap.

And as they cleaned and dusted, the mice sang a special cleaning song.

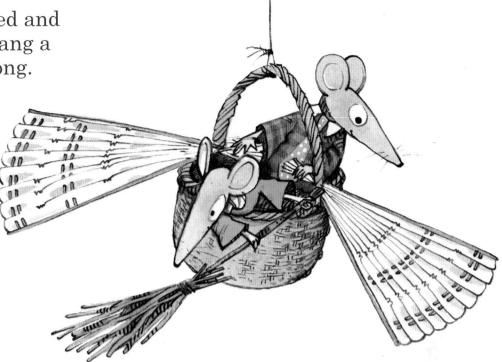

'*We will rub things, we will scrub things,*
We will make them shiny and new.
We will brush things, we will polish things,
We will make them gleam and glow.'

'Good,' said Madeleine. 'Bagpuss will like the shop to look beautiful for his birthday, but be very careful not to break anything,' she added, as Charliemouse and Janiemouse jumped into a basket and were hoisted up high to brush and dust the tops of the highest shelves.

And so that The Marvellous Mechanical Mouse
Organ would sound completely marvellous when
they all sang Happy Birthday to Bagpuss, the
mice spent extra time giving it a very special
clean. They even tightened up all the tiny
screws inside, and didn't loose any of them.

'We will dust it, we will oil it,
We will make it sing, sing, sing.
We will wipe it, we will tighten it,
We will make it ring, ring, ring.'

Sang the mice as they worked busily
and happily.

Mini Mice

'Everyone has sewn themselves for Bagpuss,' cried the mice.

Everyone except us. We want to sew us, too.'
'I haven't sewn me,' said Yaffle. 'I am just perfect as I am,
and so I don't need to make another me.'
'We don't care,' shouted the mice. 'We want to sew us!'
'Alright,' said Madeleine, 'I will help you all sew yourselves.
Then there will be lots of mice at Bagpuss's party.'

'Ridiculous,' muttered Yaffle.

'There are more than enough mice as it is!'

To make mini mice you will need...

Pattern pieces on page 47

Scraps of felt and thin cotton fabric

Pencil

Fabric scissors

Sewing needle and thread

Tiny black beads

White thread

Embroidery thread

Photocopy the pattern pieces and cut them out. Pin the body, head, back of head and arms to scraps of felt, then cut the felt pieces out.

Head

Fold the head in half and sew up one side to make a cone.

Fit the back of the head onto the open end of the cone and oversew it in place, leaving a gap at the bottom.

Body

Fold the body in half and sew up one side to make a cone. Push the point of this cone into the gap in the head and sew the pieces together.

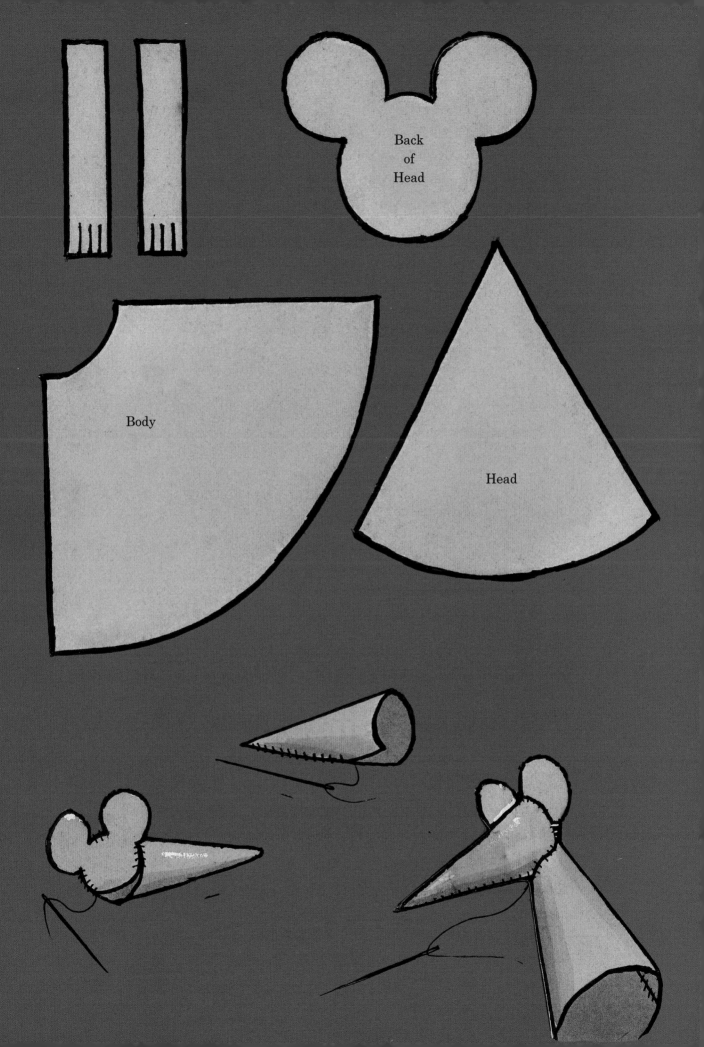

Back
of
Head

Body

Head

Arms

Fix the arms to the body by sewing or sticking them on.

Face

Sew on tiny beads for eyes, and sew lengths of white cotton through the nose to make whiskers.

Dress

Cut out the dress shape from a scrap of pretty cotton fabric. You can fray all the edges a bit if you want. Cut slits for the arms as shown on the pattern. Turn over a narrow hem at the top and sew it down along the edge. Thread a length of embroidery thread through the hem.

Put the dress on the mouse and gather the top up along the embroidery thread, then tie the thread at the back.

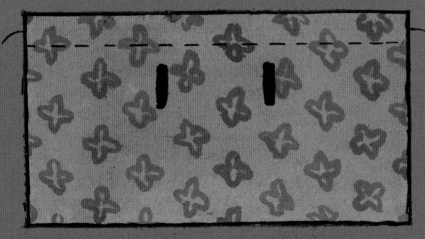

If you want to, you can make five mice and sew each one to a finger of an old glove to make finger mice puppets.

'We will snip felt, we will sew felt,

We will make many, many mice.

We will dress them, we will stitch them,

We will make pretty, pretty mice!'

Now that the shop was bright and tidy, and all the gifts were made and ready, all of the friends gathered together to celebrate Bagpuss's birthday.

'Oh my,' said Yaffle suddenly. 'I haven't made a gift for Bagpuss. I was going to, but I was so busy watching all of you, that I didn't have time. I'm sorry, Bagpuss, but I don't have a gift for you on your birthday.'

'I know what Bagpuss would like best from you, Professor Yaffle,' said Madeleine. 'A story!'

'Yes, yes,' *shouted the mice.*

'A story! Tell us a story!'

'I would like to hear a story,' agreed Bagpuss. 'I'd like an exciting story that has me as the hero. After all, it is MY birthday.'

'Ridiculous, ridiculous,' muttered Yaffle. But he settled himself down and started to tell them all a wonderful story.

It was a quiet autumn evening. All across town, the rooftops and chimney-pots gleamed softly in the light of the rising moon. Emily sat quietly in a corner of the shop, stitching a doll sleeve. Not a sound could be heard but the slow ticking of the grandfather clock.

'Tick,' went the clock.

After a while it went 'Tock.'

Another long wait, the 'Tick' again. Emily looked at it and sighed. 'What a funny old thing you are,' she said. 'It must be boring, just standing there going Tick, Tock.

Why don't you say something else for a change?'

'Tick,' went the clock, 'Tock.' It had a little model tree on its face: next to the tree was a model woodman with an axe. When the clock went 'Tick' he lifted the axe, and when it went 'Tock' he swung it down again. It was meant to look as if he was chopping down the tree, but of course it never happened. All he did was swing the axe – Tick – and back again – Tock. A swing for every Tick and every Tock, all day and all night, without stopping.

Emily wondered if the clock was happy, and whether the woodman enjoyed swinging his axe. She looked down at Bagpuss, tucked into the chair beside her, and decided it was time for him to wake up and think some magic thoughts. She hugged him close and whispered the special words into his ear.

Bagpuss stirred. He stretched and yawned. He opened his eyes and glanced around the shop. Then he settled himself more comfortably into Emily's arms.

'Hmmm,' murmured Bagpuss, 'that was a very nice sleep.'

'Well,' said Emily, 'I would never have woken you without a good reason.'

'I'm sure you wouldn't,' said Bagpuss. He yawned again. 'What time is it?'

The grandfather clock went 'Bong' eight times. 'Ah!' said Emily. 'Eight o'clock. I'd forgotten the clock says Bong as well as Tick, Tock. But he doesn't say anything else. That's what I wanted to ask you about.'

'Oh, I see,' said Bagpuss.

'What would a clock say' – went on Emily.

'No need to explain,' said Bagpuss. 'I understand perfectly. Of course. How interesting.' He began to think of all the things a clock might say if it could talk, and before very long the magic started to happen. The grandfather clock stopped going Tick, Tock, and cleared its throat.

'Who was that?' *said Emily.*

'Me,' said the clock. 'Lovely to have a chat. I've often wanted to tell you what an interesting shop this is. And I expect the poor woodman on my face will be glad to have a rest from pretending to chop down that tree.'

'Glad?' grumbled the woodman. 'I've been swinging this axe for a hundred years. I'm worn out!' And he threw down the axe and went to sit beneath the tree. Then he felt in his pocket and pulled out something wrapped in paper.

'What's that?' asked Emily.

'My lunch sandwiches,' said the woodman. 'They'll be a bit stale by now.'

'After a hundred years? I should think they will,' said Professor Yaffle. Everybody laughed; Madeleine tittered, Gabriel croaked, and the mice squeaked and jumped about in excitement. Emily felt sorry for the woodman and handed him a few crumbs from a bar of chocolate in her bag. He was very grateful and leant back against the tree to eat them.

Suddenly the clock shouted: 'It's a minute past eight on a clear moonlit night!' Immediately, the big clock on the upstairs landing yelled back: 'You're wrong – I make it two minutes past.'

'Rubbish!' answered the grandfather clock, 'you're a minute fast.'

'Oh my goodness,' said Emily, 'this is terrible.

I've always known that clocks told the time, but now they are shouting it out whenever they feel like it. Soon every clock in town will be joining in. What can we do?'

'Nothing,' said Professor Yaffle, 'until Bagpuss goes to sleep again.'

'I'm afraid he's right,' said Bagpuss, 'and I shall never go to sleep if the clocks don't stop their noise.'

As he spoke, the noise was growing worse. All the clocks in the house were calling out and chattering to each other. Outside, Emily could hear the clock on the school roof bellowing jokes about the teachers and children, and in the distance the market clock was laughing at them with a deafening clatter of rusty chains and chimes. Last and loudest of all came the voice of the town hall clock, drowning all the others as it boomed out a song about the mayor to the tune of the Westminster chimes:

**Lock up your cakes –
Here comes the mayor!
He always takes
More than his share!
CLANG! CLANG! CLANG!**

When the town clocks heard the song they all gave a great cheer and sang it again. The clock over the draper's shop had a particularly high and penetrating voice that set Emily's teeth on edge. She was very sorry indeed about the magic she had asked Bagpuss to start for her, and she was sorrier still when the town hall and market clocks began to argue at the tops of their voices over which had the biggest hands.

'Please, Bagpuss,' she begged,

'please stop it!'

'Oh dear,' said Bagpuss, 'the magic would die away if I could sleep, but how can I? Just listen to them.'

Bagpuss was right; the noise of the clocks laughing, shouting, singing and calling out the time had become so loud that people were coming out of their houses and running about in alarm. Emily didn't know what to do, but the grandfather clock was delighted. 'Marvellous!' it roared. 'High time we clocks had a bit of fun. It's half-past eight,' he announced, 'or is it half-past nine? Who cares – I'll strike twelve o-clock for luck!' And it did, several times over.

As the night went on, Professor Yaffle, Madeleine and Gabriel managed to doze off, although it wasn't easy because the grandfather clock kept exclaiming in a huge voice: 'It's getting late – no need to stay awake just to keep me company.' Emily put her hands over her ears and soon she, too, was dozing. Bagpuss sat with his eyes open, listening to all the clocks and wondering unhappily how he would ever be able to fall asleep and stop the magic.

Meanwhile the mice were busy, as mice often are at night. They searched the shop, scampering along every shelf and behind every pile of books and in every dark corner until they found what they wanted. They brought it to Bagpuss.

'Here you are, Bagpuss,' they squeaked. 'Here is a little clock.'

'Not another one,' groaned Bagpuss.

'This clock is different,' said the mice. 'It has a soft, gentle voice and it is very shy. It has promised to sing a lullaby to send you to sleep. Sing, little clock.'

The clock blushed pink and began to sing a lullaby to the tune of 'Oranges and Lemons':

'Now it's your playtime,'

Says the clock in the daytime.

'Now is the sleep-tight-time',

Says the clock in the night-time.

The lullaby worked perfectly. Bagpuss curled up on Emily's lap. His eyes shut
and he was soon fast asleep. At once the magic faded away: one by one the clocks
all over the town lost their voices and fell silent, and the people went back to
their houses, puzzled but content.

The grandfather clock was furious. 'Here!' it said, 'what's – TICK – going on –
TOCK?' The mice giggled and danced about, happy to know that Emily would find
everything back to normal when she woke. On the grandfather clock's face, the
woodman stood and picked up his axe. 'Here we go again,' he muttered, 'another
hundred years of it.' 'Tick,' went the clock, and he lifted the axe. 'Tock,' and he
brought it down again. Tick, Tock. Up, down.

The magic had ended. The slow ticking of the grandfather clock was the only
sound in the sleeping shop. Through the window the moon touched everything
with silver light as it sailed on across the night sky.

A Bedtime Bagpuss

'It's tiring, having a birthday,' said Bagpuss, sleepily.

'After all that excitement, I need a little snooze; or maybe quite a long snooze.'

And he settled down into his cushion.
Here's a case to hold your pyjamas tidily, all ready for when you need a snooze, too.

To make a pyjama case you will need...

Pattern pieces on page 62

Paper for pattern

Paper scissors

Striped fabric, 54 x 93cm

Scrap of plain fabric

Tape measure

Fabric scissors

Sewing machine

Toy stuffing

Sewing needle and thread

Three 12mm buttons, two for eyes and one for the nose

Black embroidery thread

Embroidery needle

Enlarge the pattern pieces by measuring them out onto
plain paper; each square on the pattern represents 2.5cm
(1.5cm seam allowances have been included). Pin the
pattern pieces to the fabric with the stripes running in the
right direction, and cut out the fabric pieces.

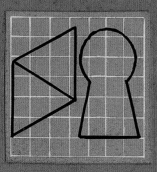

of the body. Right sides together, fold the hems to the middle,
folding on the points of the Vs in the top edge, so that the hems
overlap (you'll pop your pyjamas into the case through this gap).
Sew right around the top edge and across the bottom edge. Turn
the body right side out.

Right sides together, fold each leg and tail piece in half. Sew up one long edge and one end. Turn right side out. Turn under a little hem at the open end, then stuff. Sew up the open ends with oversewing, then sew the legs and tail in place on the body as marked on the pattern. Embroider the toes with black embroidery thread.

Sew the mouth piece onto the face as marked on the pattern: you can use zigzag stitch on the sewing machine, or you can turn under a little hem all around and sew it on by hand. Sew on the nose button at the top of the mouth piece. Embroider the mouth with black embroidery thread.

Sew on the eyes and sew eyebrows above them. These are made from little strips of fabric to contrast with the colour over the eyes, and are sewn on in the same way as the mouth piece.

Right sides together, sew the back and front of the head together, leaving an opening for stuffing. Turn right side out, stuff, and sew the opening closed.

Pin one striped and one plain ear right sides together. Sew around the sloping sides, then turn right side out. Turn under a little hem on the straight sides and oversew them closed. Sew the ears in position on the head.

Sew the head in position as marked on the pattern, slightly below the shoulder line.

When Bagpuss goes to sleep,
all his friends go to sleep, too.
The mice were ornaments on the mouse organ.
Madeleine and Gabriel were just dolls.
Professor Yaffle was a bookend...

...and even Bagpuss, once he was asleep,
was nothing but a saggy old cloth cat,
baggy and a bit loose at the seams...

...but Emily loved him.

How many things did you find beginning with B on page 36 Did you find?

Bath, bat, basin, basket, barrel, badger, bag, bagpipe, ball, balloon, banjo, barber, beads, bear, bell, bicycle, bluebell, boat, bonfire, book, boot, bottle, bow, bowl, bowler hat, boy, bread, brick, bride, bridegroom, bridge, broom, brush, bucket, budgie, bugle, bull, burglar, bust, buttercup.

The publisher would like to thank Peter and Joan Firmin, and Daniel Postgate. This book would not have been possible without their support and encouragement.

First published in the United Kingdom in 2014 by
Collins & Brown
10 Southcombe Street
London
W14 0RA

An imprint of Anova Books Company Ltd

Design and text copyright © Collins & Brown 2014

ISBN 978-1-90939-733-0

A CIP catalogue record for this book is available from the British Library.

10 9 8 7 6 5 4 3 2

Photography by Martin Norris
Reproduction by Rival Colour Ltd, UK
Printed and bound by G. Canale & C.SpA, Italy

This book can be ordered direct from the publisher at www.anovabooks.com

Join our crafting community at www.LoveCrafts.co.uk